A Selection of Old-Time Recipes for Toffee Sweets

by

Various

British Library Cataloguing-in-Publication Data
A catalogue record for this book is available from
the British Library

Toffee.—This is made a little differently by almost everyone, but the commonest recipe is the following: melt gradually over the fire 1lb. of brown sugar, 4oz. each of fresh butter and treacle, a tablespoonful of water, and the same of good vinegar, or the juice of half a lemon, and let it all cook gently together till on dropping a little into cold water it crisps and hardens at once. Now pour it into buttered plates, mark it out in squares or fingers when about half set, and leave till cold.

———— *Assafrey's.*—This is a variety of the famous Russian toffee. Put into a delicately clean pan 1lb. of brown (cane) sugar, with 4oz. butter and one tablespoonful of water; bring this all to the boil, then add a dessertspoonful of essence of vanilla and a gill of cream. Boil till on dropping it into water it will stiffen, then colour delicately with a drop or two of carmine; let it boil just two minutes longer, then lift it off the fire and let it go off the boil before pouring it into the oiled tins.

———— *Chocolate.*—Grate down ½oz. of finest French vanilla chocolate, and stir on to it gradually a gill of single cream or new milk till it forms a smooth cream; then add to it 6oz. fresh butter, 12oz. brown sugar, and a teaspoonful of treacle; boil this altogether for twenty minutes, stirring it continuously as it is apt to catch; then add a little essence of vanilla, and turn it out to cool on a buttered tin. This is never hard, but of the con-sistency of chocolate. Some people stir into it blanched and shred almonds or pistachios. Mark it out in bars, pack it in grease-proof paper, and keep it in air-tight tins.

Toffee, Everton.—Put 2lb. of not very dark brown sugar into a pan with three-quarters of a pint of water and a tiny pinch of cream of tartar, and stir it all over the fire till it boils; then put the cover on, and let it boil untouched for ten minutes in the tightly-covered pan; now test it by dropping a little into water, and if it bites sharp and clean between the teeth it is done. Have ready melted ½lb. fresh butter, flavoured with half a teaspoonful of essence of lemon; add this to the sugar, and let the butter boil well through it; then pour the toffee on to oiled or buttered tins, and mark out into bars, squares, &c., when cool.

——— *Fig.*—Boil together sugar and water, in the proportion of 1lb. of sugar to each gill of water, to the ball, then mix in 4oz. to 6oz. of sliced figs, and stir it well all the time it cooks (or it will burn) till it again comes to the ball; now add a very little carmine, and boil to the great crack (*i.e.*, till on dropping it in the cold water it crisps and tinkles as it touches the bottom of the basin), and set in oiled tins.

——— *Ginger.* — Make the toffee in the ordinary way, only adding 2oz. of ground ginger for every 1lb. of brown sugar used.

——— *Rose.*—Boil to the crack 3½lb. loaf sugar, one pint of water, and ⅛oz. of cream of tartar; colour with a very little carmine, and flavour with a few drops of otto of roses, or strong rose water, and finish off as usual. *Lemon Toffee* is made in precisely the same way, only colouring it with either saffron or apricot yellow, and flavouring it to taste with essence of lemon.

Toffee, Russian.—Make the toffee in the usual way, only using 1lb. of loaf sugar and 14oz. of cream with a teaspoonful of essence of vanilla; finish off in the usual manner, or stir into it blanched almonds or pistachios.

Everton Toffee—Boil one pound brown sugar and one half pint water until the mixture will harden when tried in cold water. Add two ounces of butter and remove from the fire. Add enough lemon extract to flavor and pour into a greased pan.

Lemon Toffee—Melt one quarter pound of butter in a saucepan, and add to it one pound of brown sugar and one half pound golden syrup. Boil over a brisk fire for twenty minutes, stirring constantly. When mixture hardens when tried in cold water, remove from fire, add enough lemon flavoring to suit taste and pour into a buttered pan.

Ginger Toffee—Prepare as in the preceding recipe, substituting a teaspoonful of Ground Ginger for the lemon extract.

Almond Toffee—To the Lemon Toffee recipe substitute vanilla extract for the lemon extract and just before pouring into a buttered tin add two ounces and a half of chopped blanched sweet almonds.

Soft Toffee—Melt two ounces of butter in a

saucepan. To it add one cup milk, or cream, one half can condensed milk, and one pound brown sugar and allow to boil twenty-five minutes. Stir in one teaspoon vanilla and three ounces walnuts, and pour into a greased platter.

English Toffee—To two cups sugar add one and one half cups corn syrup, one and one half cups thin cream, and a liberal pinch of salt. Stir until the boiling point is reached. Continue cooking, stirring occasionally, until the mixture forms a firm ball when tried in cold water. Add four tablespoons butter and cook again until the mixture forms a hard ball when tried in cold water. Add one teaspoon vanilla extract before removing from the fire. Pour into a well buttered pan or platter and mark into rectangular shapes. The creases should be quite deep so as to allow the candy to be separated easily. Wrap each piece in waxed paper.

American Toffee—To one-half cup of brown sugar, add one-half cup corn syrup, one-half cup white sugar, one-half cup of rich cream, and stir over a brisk fire until the boiling point is reached. Wash down any sugar which might adhere to the sides of the saucepan with a damp cheese cloth. When nearly cooked add two tablespoons butter; when the mixture becomes a hard ball when tried in cold water, remove from fire, add a liberal pinch of salt, one-half teaspoon vanilla extract, and one-half cup of chopped English walnuts. Pour into a well buttered pan, and cut in pieces one inch wide by one and a half inches long.

Lollypops—Put two cups of sugar, two-thirds cup corn syrup, and one cup of water in a saucepan, and stir over a brisk fire until the mixture becomes brittle when tried in cold water. During the cooking wash off any sugar crystals which might adhere to the sides of the saucepan with a damp cloth. When done, remove from fire, add the coloring desired and eight drops oil of peppermint or any other flavoring, and stir only enough to mix. From the tip of a spoon drop the syrup on a buttered slab or an inverted platter. Press one end of a skewer into the edge of each lollypop. For larger lollypops pour the syrup from the pan. The work should be done very quickly as the syrup hardens very rapidly. Wrap in waxed paper.

Molasses Mint Toffee—Mix together two teaspoons of vinegar and two cups of molasses. Boil slowly until the mixture becomes hard when tried in cold water. Remove from fire, add three tablespoons butter, one-half teaspoon soda, and a liberal pinch of salt. Beat until the syrup is free from lumps and ceases to foam. Pour into a well buttered platter. When cool enough to handle, pour five drops oil of peppermint into the center of the mass and then pull until the candy becomes light in color and rather firm. Stretch in a long rope and cut with shears. Wrap in waxed paper.

TOFFEES

As a general rule toffee has a perfectly smooth appearance, therefore the grain of the sugar must be cut, and every precaution taken to prevent it from becoming sugary.

RULES FOR TOFFEE-MAKING

1 Follow Rules for Sugar Boiling (p. 29). Always boil toffee in a saucepan of a capacity larger than the quantity actually needs at first, as these mixtures boil over very quickly.

2 If the mixture is inclined to boil over, brush the inside top of the saucepan with olive oil or oiled butter.

3 As a general rule, avoid stirring toffees—the exceptions to this rule being such toffees as Scotch or Russian toffee, which are of different texture, and where slow stirring is specially directed.

4 Lower the flame after 260° F. has been reached ; if the flame is too strong against the bottom of the pan at this stage the syrup will be scorched and the toffee will taste bitter.

5 While boiling, occasionally change the position of the thermometer gently, as the thermometer checks free bubbling where it stands, thus the mixture is more likely to burn at that spot.

6 Draw off the saucepan 5° below the required point, or the heat in the toffee may cause the mixture to be overboiled. See that the syrup runs up to the correct degree.

7 Always allow the bubbles to die down before pouring out the toffee.

8 Always warm the nuts to be added to hot toffee ; if added cold they may cause it to granulate.

9 When cut, wipe the toffees lightly with soft paper to remove any oil, and place the pieces on greaseproof paper until perfectly cold.

10 Wrap each piece of toffee in waxed tissue paper to prevent

the pieces sticking together. If required for storing, a further wrapping of tinfoil should be used.

Note : Store toffees in an airtight tin in a cool dry place.

TO FINISH TOFFEES

IN CUSHIONS

It is advisable to put half the mixture aside in a lightly oiled warm tin in a warm place while dealing with the remainder.

To Cut the Cushions :

Roll the mixture into cylinders of about 6 in. long by $\frac{1}{2}$ in. to $\frac{3}{4}$ in. diameter, and cut these rolls with a pair of oiled scissors into pieces (or cushions) $\frac{1}{2}$ in. to $\frac{3}{4}$ in. long.

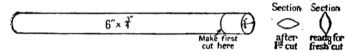

Note : It will be seen that after each cut the end of the cylinder becomes pointed ; therefore, after each piece is cut, half turn the cylinder so that the point comes to the top. This half-turn in cutting gives the pieces their familiar cushion shape.

To Wrap the Cushions :

Cushions should be wrapped in paper with cracker ends :
(*a*) Put each cushion on a square of paper with about 2 in. margin on each side of it.
(*b*) Turn in $\frac{1}{4}$ in. of the paper to make a neat edge on the farther side from the worker, and roll up the cushion.
(*c*) Finish the projecting ends of the package by giving these a twist forward on one side, and in the reverse direction on the other.
(*d*) These turns should be made very close to the cushion, and the ends well spread. Of course, facility in wrapping comes with practice.

IN BARS

(*a*) Arrange the candy bars in a narrow oblong of about 3 in. to 3½ in. depth by width as required. The toffee may then be marked in strips 1 in. wide, thus avoiding a transverse cutting.
(*b*) When pouring out toffee between candy bars, or into an oiled tin, begin at one end, pass steadily down to the other, pouring meanwhile, and avoid repassing.
(*c*) Do not add the scrapings of the pan to the batch, as this would spoil the appearance, and would be liable to crystallise the toffee.
(*d*) When half cold, remove the bars, and mark the toffee heavily into strips with the back of a knife, or press firmly with an oiled caramel marker if required in squares.
(*e*) Cut the bars alternately from either end, as the centre of the batch holds the heat longest.
Note : It is very important to watch toffee carefully while it is cooling, in order to cut it at the right moment. If cut when too hot it will spread in all directions, and if allowed to become too cold the toffee will splinter, and it will not be possible to obtain a clean cut.
(*f*) When cutting toffee hold the oiled knife very lightly, and cut quickly with a sawing motion. This is to give a sharp edge to the bars.

IN DROPS

(*a*) Lightly oil the slab, or a large dish, and stand the sweet rings upon it which have been oiled inside.
(*b*) Pour the boiled toffee into each ring evenly to the required depth, which is usually about ⅛ in. to ¼ in.
(*c*) When set, lift each ring, and remove the toffee by tapping smartly, or ease with a small pointed knife.

IN TINS

If no candy bars are available pour toffee into a shallow tin lined with oiled greaseproof paper. A tin of about 9 in. by 5 in. is suitable for toffee made from 1 lb. sugar, etc., or 12 in. by 4 in. is convenient if the toffee is to be cut into bars.

After about 10 minutes, mark the toffee into 1 in. strips, and when set, but not cold, invert the toffee from the tin, peel off the paper, and complete the cutting. Either leave in bars, or cut across into 1 in. squares.

FAMILY TOFFEE

1 *lb. Demerara sugar*	*Large pinch of cream of tartar*
1¼ *gills water*	2 *oz. brown treacle, golden syrup or*
2 *oz. butter*	*plain malt extract*
	2 *teaspoons vinegar*

1 Dissolve the sugar in the water. Add the butter, cream of tartar, treacle and vinegar and boil up.
2 Boil just steadily to 280° F. or until a little of the toffee dropped into a cup of cold water breaks with a snap.
3 Withdraw from heat, and, when the bubbles have died down, finish in bars or squares and wrap each piece in waxed tissue paper.

NUT TOFFEE

1 *lb. Demerara sugar*	1 *dessertspoon glucose*
1¼ *gills water*	2 *oz. fresh butter*
	2 *oz. chopped prepared nuts*

1 Dissolve the sugar in the water, following Rules for Sugar Boiling (p. 29).
2 Add the glucose and the butter, and boil to 285° F., following Rules for Toffees.
3 Pour the mixture out upon an oiled slab, and scatter the roughly chopped nuts over.
4 Fold the batch over with an oiled knife, and divide the mixture into two portions.
5 Cut into cushions (p. 64), and finish in waxed paper with cracker ends.

Note : (*a*) Suitable nuts for use in this toffee are : dried walnut halves, blanched browned almonds, roasted peanuts, skinned and roughly chopped Brazil nuts, or desiccated coconut. If the latter is used, 1 oz. will be found sufficient.

(b) Treacle Toffee or Molasses Toffee may be made by adding 1 tablespoon of treacle or molasses to the above ingredients after the sugar has dissolved, omitting the glucose, and substituting a large pinch of cream of tartar. In this case the nuts are usually omitted.

FRENCH ALMOND ROCK

1 *lb. Demerara sugar*	*A pinch cream of tartar*
1¼ *gills water*	2–4 *oz. butter*
1 *dessertspoon glucose*	2–4 *oz. blanched browned almonds*
	A few drops almond essence

1 Dissolve the sugar in the water, following Rules for Sugar Boiling (p. 29).
2 Add the glucose, cream of tartar and butter, and boil to 285° F., following Rules for Toffees (p. 63).
3 Remove to table, add the almond essence, and shake the saucepan slightly to mix it in. *N.B.*—Do not stir the mixture.
4 Pour out one-third of the mixture on an oiled slab between bars, add the prepared nuts to the remainder, and pour on top.
5 Finish in bars.

'BUTTERED' ALMONDS AND WALNUTS

½ *lb. Demerara sugar*	*A pinch cream of tartar*
¾ *gill water*	2 *oz. butter*
1 *teaspoon glucose*	1 *oz. blanched browned almonds*
	1 *oz. dried walnut halves*

1 Dissolve the sugar in the water, following Rules for Sugar Boiling (p. 29).
2 When dissolved add the glucose, cream of tartar and the butter.
3 Boil, following Rules for Toffee, to 285° F.
4 Place warmed nuts at intervals on a lightly oiled slab with an oiled sweet ring over each.
5 Finish in drops (p. 65).

Alternative Method of Finishing :

When the bubbles have died down, and the toffee is slightly thickened by cooling, drop three or four nuts into it, and lift each out singly with a teaspoon, turning the spoon so that the toffee flows evenly around the nut. This method is the one which is most suitable for buttered Brazils, as these nuts, if left whole, would not fit into sweet rings.

CLEAR NUT TOFFEE

1 *lb. granulated sugar*	*A large teaspoon glucose*
1¼ *gills water*	¼ *lb. prepared nuts*
A pinch cream of tartar	*Vanilla or almond essence to taste*

1 Dissolve the sugar in the water, following Rules for Sugar Boiling (p. 29).
2 Add the glucose and the cream of tartar dissolved in a little water, and boil to 300° F., following Rules for Toffees.
3 Spread the prepared warmed nuts on a slab between candy bars, and pour the boiled toffee over.
4 Finish in bars.

Note : The most suitable nuts for use in this toffee are blanched almonds, split transversely, and browned ; dried walnut halves or quarters, or pignolia kernels.

EVERTON TOFFEE

1 *lb. loaf or granulated sugar*	*Scant ½ gill golden syrup*
1¼ *gills water*	½ *teaspoon lemon essence*
3–4 *oz. butter*	*A large pinch cream of tartar*

1 Dissolve the sugar in the water, following Rules for Sugar Boiling (p. 29).
2 Add the syrup, one-third of the butter, cream of tartar, and boil in the usual way to 260° F.
3 Add the remainder of the butter, cutting it in thin slices and boiling it quickly into the toffee.
4 Boil very carefully to 300° F., stirring occasionally and very gently with the thermometer after 260° F.

5 Remove to table, then add the lemon essence.
6 Finish in bars, making the batch ½ in. thick.

Note : When well made this toffee stores well.

BUTTER SCOTCH

1 *lb. loaf or granulated sugar*	¼ *teaspoon cream of tartar*
1¼ *gills water*	½ *teaspoon vanilla essence*
	2–3 *oz. butter*

1 Dissolve the sugar in the water in the usual way.
2 When dissolved add cream of tartar. Boil to 240° F.
3 Add the butter, cutting it in thin slices.
4 Cook, following Rules for Toffees (p. 63), until a little sets
hard and crisp when dropped into some cold water, 280° F.
5 Add the essence just before the batch is ready.
6 Finish in bars or squares, making the batch ¼ in. thick.

Note : It is better to mark butter scotch deeply, then leave
it until quite cold and hard before breaking up.

TO MAKE RICH BUTTER SCOTCH

Ingredients and method as above, but use the larger quantity
of butter, and add 1 gill fresh cream, or cream and milk,
when dissolving, which latter should be done very slowly.

BARLEY SUGAR

| 1 *lb. loaf or granulated sugar* | 6 *lumps of sugar* |
| 1½ *gills water* | *Zest and juice of half a lemon* |

1 Rub the six lumps of sugar on the lemon to remove
the zest.
2 Put these in a saucepan with the remainder of the sugar
and the water.
3 Dissolve slowly, following Rules for Sugar Boiling (p. 29).
4 When the syrup is quite clear boil to 270° F., and add
the lemon juice.
5 Boil carefully to 300° F., allowing the mixture to reach

this degree *very slowly*. The syrup should be a pale straw colour at this stage.

6 Pour out thinly on an oiled slab.

7 When slightly cooled, cut in even strips and twist.

8 Place on greaseproof paper, and as soon as the sticks are cool pack in airtight tins or jars, as barley sugar quickly becomes soft when exposed to the air.

PEPPERMINT TOFFEE

1 *lb. loaf or granulated sugar*	*A large pinch cream of tartar*
¼ *lb. dark brown sugar*	1 *teaspoon glucose*
1¾ *gills water*	1½ *oz. butter*

1–2 *large teaspoons peppermint essence (according to strength),*
or a few drops oil of peppermint

1 Put both sugars in a saucepan and dissolve them in the water, following Rules for Sugar Boiling (p. 29).

2 Add the glucose and the cream of tartar, and boil to 240° F.

3 Add the oiled butter, or cut it in fine flakes and add these one at a time to the boiling syrup.

4 Boil carefully, following Rules for Toffees, to 300° F. (p. 63).

5 Add the peppermint essence, and finish in bars or drops.

PEPPERMINT CUSHIONS

1 *lb. granulated sugar*	1½ *oz. butter*
1¼ *gills water*	1 *large tablespoon glucose*

1–2 *large teaspoons peppermint essence (according to strength), or a few drops oil of peppermint*

1 Dissolve the sugar in the water, following Rules for Sugar Boiling (p. 29).

2 Add the glucose, and boil to 240° F.

3 Oil the butter, and add it to the boiling syrup, or add it in fine flakes one at a time.

4 Continue boiling carefully until the temperature of the mixture reaches 290° F.

5 Pour out on an oiled slab, and frequently fold the edges of the mixture over with an oiled knife to keep it together. Add essence or oil.

6 As soon as the mixture is cool enough to handle, pull by hand or over a candy hook until quite white and opaque.

7 Finish in cushions.

Note : The cushions should taste strongly of peppermint.

HARDBAKE

1 *lb. Demerara sugar*	3 *teaspoons glucose*
1¼ *gills water*	2 *oz. butter*
A large pinch cream of tartar	4–6 *oz. almonds*

1 Dissolve the sugar in the water, following Rules for Sugar Boiling (p. 29).

2 Blanch the almonds, split transversely, and dry thoroughly without browning.

3 Add the butter, glucose and cream of tartar to the syrup.

4 Bring to boiling point, and boil steadily to 300° F., or until very dark in colour.

5 Pour out on an oiled slab between bars, and sprinkle the almonds over the toffee evenly.

6 Leave the mixture until quite set, then break up in rough pieces.

BULL'S-EYES

1 *lb. Demerara sugar*	*A pinch cream of tartar*
1¼ *gills water*	*A large pinch tartaric acid*
1 *teaspoon peppermint or lemon essence*	

1 Dissolve the sugar in the water, following Rules for Sugar Boiling (p. 29).

2 Add the cream of tartar, and boil, following Rules for Toffees, to 290° F. (p. 63).

3 Pour out on an oiled slab, cut off one-third of the mixture, and pull until creamy white. Keep remainder warm in an oiled tin.

4 Add the essence and tartaric acid to the remainder. At

this stage some coffee brown colouring may be added if a darker colour is desired.

5 Take the pulled part and draw it out in lengths. Make the brown part into a roll. Either (a) lay the white portion on the brown one in two strips, 1 in. apart in the centre, and fold the roll over so that the strips show on both sides and the two ends of the brown roll are brought together ; or (b) twist the white length around the brown roll.

6 Keep rolling the combined mixture until quite round and well pressed together, then cut into convenient-sized pieces with a pair of oiled scissors.

Note : Great speed and dexterity are necessary in the management of the portions, as if either portion becomes too hard, a proper blending cannot be effected. Work in a warm place, avoiding draughts.

RUSSIAN TOFFEE

1 *lb. castor sugar*	¼ *lb. butter*
½ *gill cream or top milk*	¼ *lb. honey*
¾ *gill water*	*Lemon essence*
1 *dessertspoon glucose*	*Carmine*

1 Dissolve the sugar in the cream and water slowly.
2 Add the glucose, honey, and one-third of the butter, and dissolve.
3 Boil to 240° F., stirring slowly all the time.
4 Add the remainder of the butter, cutting it in thin slices so that it may boil quickly through the syrup.
5 Add sufficient carmine to tinge the toffee.
6 Boil slowly and carefully to 280° F.
7 Add lemon essence to taste.
8 Pour out and finish in bars.

Note : (a) Russian Toffee requires careful cooking throughout. It is safer to stand the saucepan on an asbestos mat.
(b) Stir the toffee *slowly and gently* throughout the process.

SCOTCH TOFFEE

1 *lb. granulated sugar*   2 *oz. butter*
1¼ *gills water*   1 *teaspoon vanilla essence*
    1 *small tin sweetened condensed milk*

1 Dissolve the sugar in the water, following Rules for Sugar Boiling (p. 29).
2 Add the butter and condensed milk, and dissolve them well in the syrup.
3 Boil to 250° F., stirring gently meanwhile.
4 Add the vanilla essence, and pour out the mixture between bars on an oiled slab.
5 When setting, press with a well-oiled caramel marker, and cut into squares when cold.

YORKSHIRE BUTTER TOFFEE

1 *lb. Demerara sugar*   1 *dessertspoon glucose*
1¼ *gills water*   3 *oz. fresh butter*
    Lemon or vanilla essence

1 Dissolve the sugar in the water, following Rules for Sugar Boiling (p. 29).
2 Add the glucose and one-third of the butter. Boil up, and boil to 240° F.
3 Add the remainder of the butter in thin flakes, one at a time, allowing each flake to boil into the toffee quite undisturbed. Boil gently to 285° F.
4 Remove the pan to the table, and add the essence chosen, sprinkling it over the surface. Twist the pan in rotary fashion once or twice to mingle the essence, but do not stir.
5 Pour out on to an oiled slab between bars, and when sufficiently set cut into 1 in. bars. Wrap in waxed tissue paper, and store in an airtight tin when cold.

CHOCOLATE TOFFEE

1 *scant lb. golden syrup*	¼ *lb. plain chocolate*
1 *lb. granulated sugar*	2–3 *oz. butter*

1 Heat the golden syrup gently in a saucepan, stirring from time to time to prevent burning. Withdraw from heat, and add the sugar.

2 Dissolve the sugar in the syrup, stirring slowly, and occasionally, brushing down with warm water if crystals are deposited above the level of the mixture.

3 When the sugar has completely dissolved, add the butter cut in small pieces, and the chocolate which has been scraped finely with a knife.

4 When the butter and chocolate are dissolved, increase the heat somewhat, and boil to 290° F. stirring gently and occasionally with the thermometer.

5 When the bubbles have died down, pour the toffee on to an oiled slab between candy bars, and when sufficiently set score deeply into ¾ in. bars with the back of an oiled knife, and cut into squares when almost cold.

6 Wrap each square in waxed tissue paper, and store in a tin when cold.

HONEYCOMB TOFFEE

½ *lb. granulated sugar*	2 *level teaspoons bicar-*
½ *lb. golden syrup*	*bonate of soda, dissolved*
3 *tablespoons water*	*in* 1 *tablespoon warm*
½ *teaspoon glucose, or a*	*water*
pinch of cream of tartar	2 *oz. butter*

1 Dissolve the sugar in the golden syrup and water. Add the butter cut into pieces, and the glucose or cream of tartar.

2 Boil up and boil approximately 10 minutes without stirring, until a rich brown colour (310° F.).

3 Remove pan from heat, and while still boiling stir the dissolved soda through, lightly and quickly.

4 While still frothing, pour the toffee on to an oiled slab between bars, or into an oiled tin.

5 When almost firm and still slightly warm, loosen the edges and cut up.

6 Store in an airtight tin immediately it is cold, as this toffee becomes sticky more quickly than most others.

Lightning Source UK Ltd.
Milton Keynes UK
UKOW041934091112

201974UK00001B/152/P